Ackn owle dgments

It would be impossible for me to write Automatic and not use this space to express my extreme gratitude to those who helped me complete the assignment that God required of me.

I must first thank my Lord and Savior Jesus Christ. I publicly declare that You are the head of my life and the source of my strength.

To my incredible wife and best friend, Tracy. I hope you remember this. We were in church one Sunday and our pastor asked us to turn to our neighbor sitting next to us, look them in their eyes, and repeat this phrase, "I see greatness in you." I remember that as we said these words to each other, both of our eyes filled with tears. Every day that I look into your eyes, I am blessed to see the greatest and most beautiful gift that God has given me. Thank you for always taking the time to read and re-read and re-read chapters I had written and giving me honest feedback. Thank you for seeing greatness in me and standing beside me in love and support.

To my son, Aswin, Jr. Writing a book is tough and time-consuming. Some of the best escapes from writing were watching you kick butt on the football field, ride a roller coaster, or eat a burrito from your favorite restaurant. You are incredibly smart, and your mother and I are so proud of you. You are the reason that I have the blessing of being called Dad.

To my mother, Willie Pinkney. There is no chance that I will sum up the impact you have made in my life in just a few sentences. Any skill I possess for writing I must attribute to you. For as long as I can remember, you were a stickler who required that I used proper grammar when writing and proper diction when speaking. Using slang and poor grammar was not an option around you. As much as I may have wanted to come home from school and say, "Yo, Mamma, what up?" I knew you required more of me. I have become an author and a public speaker because you made me accountable for what I write and how I speak. Your requirement for proper diction and grammar pale in comparison to your requirement that I come to know Jesus as my Lord and Savior. I could dive into using slang when you were not around, but I could never escape the lessons you taught me about the Lord. I am most grateful to you for these lessons that have helped to shape me into the man I am today. Thank you!

To my dad, John Johnson, Sr. You are one of the funniest people on the planet. I so cherish the relationship we have now. Whenever we are together and for no reason at all, you tell me you are proud of me and you like hanging out with me. This means a lot. Thank you!

To my uncle, Bishop JR Pinkney. You have remained incredibly supportive and I am grateful for your timely wisdom, prayers, and encouragement. I am also grateful for your friendship. The Bible says in Proverbs 27:17, "As iron sharpens iron, so one person sharpens another." Thank you for helping me on my journey to become razor sharp.

To my uncle, Reggie Pinkney. You always ask me, "How is the book coming?" On one occasion, I let you know I had written nothing in over a month because I was busy with work for my job and other obligations. You sensed the disappointment in my voice, and you asked me, "Did God tell you to write this book?" When I replied, "Yes," you said, "Well, pray and ask Him to supply you with the time and resources to accomplish what He told you to do." That very night, I went to God in prayer and He supplied me with everything I needed to finish, Automatic. Thank you!

To my brother, Jay Johnson. A great writer. Thank you for being willing to read anything I put in front of you. Your endorsement and encouragement have given me confidence as a writer.

To my sister. Latisha Rasheem. Thank you for your support. I love having a little sister. For so many years it was just me and Jay and I was the little brother. Then you came along and now I have someone to pick on.

To Collier Rowe, Sr. You are more than just my brother-in-law. You are my brother. Thank you for always having my back. If I am ever forced to fight a bear, I know that from an extremely safe distance, you will cheer me on.

To my pastor, Dr. Mark E. Whitlock, Jr. Pastor Mark, you are the reason I wrote Automatic. My wife and I met with you in your office to ask you some questions. After listening to our questions, you asked me some hard questions. Two of the questions were, "Where is your book? Why are you not writing a book?" I immediately knew God was using you to give me the push I needed to write Automatic. Thank you!

To Pastor Sheryl Menendez. Thank you for always being excited to see me. I also want to thank you for meeting with me and allowing God to use you to pray an incredible prayer that has covered my ministry and my family. Thank you!

To Beverly Askia at Glad Tidings Bookstore. Thank you so much for your kindness, encouragement, and for walking me through this entire process. Working with you speaks volumes about how God's people, even in business, should treat each other. Thank you!

CONTENTS

CHAPTER 1

Mr. Nerd

"No temptation has overtaken you except what is common to
mankind. And God is faithful; he will not let you be tempted
beyond what you can bear. But when you are tempted, he will
also provide a way out so that you can endure it."

–1 Corinthians 10:13 (NIV)

Where was 1 Corinthians 10:13 when I was thirteen years old and was a student in Mr. Nerd's class? A strong temptation overtook me, and I gave into it! Mr. Nerd was my eighth-grade science teacher. His actual name was not Mr. Nerd. I cannot remember it, but his parents should have named him Mr. Nerd because that was exactly what he was—a NERD! Grab a dictionary right now and look up nerd and I can almost promise you his picture will be right there, figuratively. Every day, he wore all the prerequisite clothes that made him a super nerd. He wore big glasses with large thick lenses. When he looked at you with those thick glasses, his eyeballs were the size of watermelons. He always wore the required white short-sleeved dress shirt, with a bowtie, and a pocket protector. He always pulled his pants up high above his waist, exposing dingy white baseball socks. The black dress shoes he wore were a complete mess—oddly shaped, the front dull with scuff marks—but the backs of his shoes were polished. When I looked at his shoes, I always wanted to ask him how he scuffed up the front of his shoes so badly but kept the backs of his shoes looking great. I never really liked Mr. Nerd. His class was super boring and instead of paying attention in class, I found it more fun to talk to my friends.

One day, Mr. Nerd was teaching a mind-numbing lesson on photosynthesis. My seat was toward the back of the class, so instead of listening, I was talking to my friends. Mr. Nerd became upset, and said, "Aswin, stand up and tell me and the entire class the definition of photosynthesis!"

I had no idea; I was not paying attention at all. "Well," I paused and cleared my throat, "photosynthesis is when you take a photo and synthesize it together." Of course, this was not the correct definition of photosynthesis and the class erupted in laughter, and because they were laughing, I laughed, too.

Mr. Nerd became furious. He screamed, "No! Aswin, photosynthesis is the process in which green plants use sunlight to make their own food. You would know this if you had not been talking and had been paying attention! And since you were not paying attention, I am going to give you a detention and you can stay after school with me today and read all about photosynthesis in your textbook for an hour!"

He stopped teaching, went to his desk, and pulled out a detention form. This explained to your parents that your behavior caused you to receive detention you had to serve after school with the teacher. It also explained whatever you did wrong, and included the school's phone number, in case your parents wanted to discuss the issue. The worst part of this form was that parent's signature was required to acknowledge they knew their child had received detention.

Mr. Nerd wrote on the form that I was excessively talking in class and when he confronted me about talking in class, I disrupted the entire class and started laughing about disrupting the class. Serving the detention was going to be the easy part. I could put up with Mr. Nerd and his nerdy ways for an hour after school. Besides, I was used to staying after school because, on certain days, I would play pick-up basketball games in the gym. However, I was more worried about giving my mother that detention form. If I were to give her that form, she would kill me. Her reading that I was "excessively talking" and I had "disrupted the entire class" and then "laughed about it," would spell the end for me. Rather, the last time I would sit down for at least the next week because I was surely going to get a big-time spanking.

A huge temptation came over me that day—serve the detention and give my mother the detention form to sign, which was the right thing to do, and suffer the consequences, or serve the detention and forge my mother's signature on the form and never tell her about it. Signing her name was wrong, that much I knew, and I had just gotten saved and accepted Jesus Christ as my Lord and Savior a few weeks earlier. Lying was wrong and forging her signature was wrong, but the temptation to do wrong was so strong. It was too strong! I served the detention and forged her signature on the detention form. This would be a terrible decision.

After school that day, I reported to Mr. Nerd's class to serve my detention. Spending an hour with Mr. Nerd was not as bad as I thought it would have been. He was no longer upset with me, and he explained why my actions had caused him to give me a detention. He told me he knew how smart I was and if I would just focus and stop talking all the time, I could be a good student. Then he explained photosynthesis to me. He gave me some tips to help me study for the upcoming test. He also asked about my favorite sports team, and we talked about that for a minute before he allowed me to leave detention early.

You know, at that moment, I was feeling differently about Mr. Nerd. I figured I should probably stop talking and start paying attention in his class. It might also be a good idea to learn his real name and to stop laughing at his weird-looking shoes. I was seeing the light…that is until he said one last thing as I was walking out of his classroom.

"Be sure to get your mother to sign that detention form and bring it back to me tomorrow."

Wow! I had forgotten about that. Just when I was making a connection with Mr. Nerd, he brought up that detention form, and my stress level soared through the roof.

Looking back at him, I gave him a thumbs-up, and said, "Okay," even though I had already decided to forge my mother's signature. Confident I could mimic the way my mother signed her name, I stuffed the detention form in my bookbag. I would sign the form on the bus the next morning heading to school. This way, once I got home, if I decided to do what was right, then I could just give my mother the form and suffer the consequences.

When I got home from school and walked in the door, I heard the anger in my mother's voice as she talked on the phone. Why was my mother home so early from work? I immediately froze and tuned my supersonic ears in her direction. Oh, my gosh! I thought, Is she on the phone with Mr. Nerd? Listening intently, I wanted to make sure she was not on the phone with him. It would have infuriated and terrified me if he had called my mother after we had gotten to know each other better at detention. Thank you, Jesus! As I listened closer, my mother was talking with one of her co-workers. She was angry about something that had happened at work.

"I know. They get on my last nerves, too, and that's why I left early. Well, girl, we are going to be all right. I will talk to you tomorrow. My son just walked in from school."

"Hey, Ma!" This was my usual greeting when I came home from school and my mother was already there.

We exchanged pleasantries, and she told me to get started on my homework. I was so relieved; Mr. Nerd did not call her, and she did not question why I was home late from school. I just had to sign her name to the detention form in the morning before school and everything would be all right.

The next morning, my focus was on the mission at hand. My mom had already left for work and my brother, Jay, who was in high school, was just about to leave to catch his bus. Jay was my best friend, and I usually ran everything past him, but I decided not to tell him about the detention and my plan to forge my mother's signature on the form.

I got dressed for school and grabbed a ballpoint pen from my mother's nightstand. She always signed her name in black ink with a ballpoint pen. I dashed out the door to catch the bus. In hindsight, I should have signed the detention form at my house before I left for school, but I chose to sign it on the bus. Our bus was usually quiet in the morning because everyone was still half asleep, so I figured this would be a good place and time to sign the form. I pulled it out and looked around to see if anybody was watching me. The coast was clear, so I took out the pen. My mother always signed her name using the first initial of her first name, then her middle initial, and finally she wrote out her last name. Her signature was *W. L. Pinkney*. My parents were divorced, and my mother was now using her maiden name. I started trying to write the *W.*, and nothing happened. "You have got to be kidding me!" The one pen I grabbed from my mother's nightstand was out of ink. Shaking the pen, trying to get just enough ink so I could write *W. L. Pinkney*, all I got was a speck of ink to puddle at the tip of the ballpoint pen. I crossed my fingers that this would be enough. I should have crossed my toes, too, because that speck of ink was only enough for me to write the *W.* I shook the pen again, but it did not matter. It was out of ink. What was I going to do? I knew there was no point in waking up someone on the bus to see if they had an ink pen because we could not write in ink at school. We were only allowed to write with a #2 pencil. I left the *W.* as I had written it with the speck of ink, and I signed L. Pinkney in pencil. I convinced myself that it was perfectly reasonable for Mr. Nerd to believe that as my mother began to sign her signature, her ballpoint pen ran out of ink after signing the *W.* and she did not have another ink pen, so she signed the remainder of her signature with a #2 pencil. Makes sense to me. So I signed the rest of my mother's signature in pencil. I signed the *L.* and that looked pretty good.

When I started signing *Pinkney*, the bus driver hit a big pothole in the road, causing me to press down too hard on the paper. The sharp tip of the pencil poked a big hole in the paper. "Oh, no!" Now there was a pothole sized hole in the paper exactly where I needed to sign my mother's last name. I ignored the hole and signed *Pinkney* next to the big hole. It looked a complete mess like a five-year-old had signed this paper and not my mother.

Now, I know what you are probably saying, "Aswin, you couldn't have turned that detention form in looking like that," and my reply to you is, "I had no choice." The school policy regarding detention forms stated that once the detention was served, the detention form must be signed the next day by a parent or guardian or the teacher must call the parent or guardian to ask why the form was not signed and returned. So, if I did not turn in the form, I knew Mr. Nerd would, without hesitation, call my mother at work.

As soon as I walked into the classroom, Mr. Nerd said, "Good morning, Aswin, do you have something for me?"

I knew I had to play it cool. If I acted nervously or showed any sign of weakness, Mr. Nerd would have known my mother did not sign that form. I confidently said, "Yes, sir, I have a signed detention form for you." I just did not tell him I was the one who signed it. I gave him the form and took my seat. He did not even look at it. He put it in a pile of papers sitting on his desk and that was it. We had class as usual and, of course, I was on my best behavior. I was so relieved my plan worked!

When I got home from school, my mother was not home yet, so I called her at work just to make sure Mr. Nerd had not called her. I was nervous as I used our rotary telephone to dial her work number. As I dialed 301-555-4100 my hand was sweating and I was shaking like a leaf. My mother's co-worker, Ms. Whitt, answered the phone. Ms. Whitt was fond of me, and she was excited to hear from me. After we talked for a minute, I asked her if I could speak to my mother. I was planning to ask my mother a simple question, like "Could I have a few cookies out of the cookie jar?" or ask her "What are we having for dinner?" I just wanted to see if Mr. Nerd had called her.

After Ms. Whitt put me on hold, she came back on the line. "Your mother told me to tell you that she is busy at the moment and she will talk to you later."

I said goodbye to Ms. Whitt, and we hung up.

Now I was nervous. Was my mother really "busy at the moment" or was she so mad at that moment because that super nerd, Mr. Nerd, had called her about my forging her signature and she just said she was "busy at the moment" because she wanted to deal with me in person? I was a complete nervous wreck for the next three hours. That was how long it would be until my mother came home. I did not want to eat anything. I did not want to watch

TV. I did not want to go outside and play basketball. I did not want to do anything until I found out if my mother knew what I had done. I am not sure how I passed the time for the next three hours.

Around 7:00 p.m., I heard my mother's key insert into the front door. I raced into the bathroom and shut the door. My heart was racing so fast. Then, my mother called my name, and I knew Mr. Nerd had made the phone call.

"Aswin, hurry up and get your butt out of that bathroom right now!"

It never had to come to this. I should have told my mother about the detention. Instead, when temptation told me not to tell her, to forge her signature, and just turn it into Mr. Nerd, I gave in to the temptation and did what I knew was wrong! Of course, you can guess how this story ends. I wasn't able to sit down on my rear end for what seemed like the next week because I gave in to temptation.

CHAPTER 2

Addictions, Strongholds, and Temptations

Every Christian is going to have to deal with temptation. 1 Corinthians 10:13 says temptation is common. It may surprise you, but only a Christian, someone who has experienced a spiritual new birth that only God can deliver, can be tempted. You might question this, but what is temptation? A temptation is an enticement that leads you away from the will of God. You cannot be led away from God if you never belonged to God. The first step to dealing with and overcoming temptation is being able to answer the question of if you belong to God. You must be able to answer definitively if you are saved. Have you been born again? Have you been made alive in Christ? Do you have a personal relationship and friendship with our Lord and Savior Jesus Christ? If you can answer yes to these questions, I suggest you keep on reading. I believe this book will be a great blessing to you as you

19

learn to defeat temptation. If you cannot answer yes, I believe it is not by chance or luck that you are reading this book. I believe that almighty God wants to offer you the greatest gift you could ever receive. He wants to save you from sin (breaking His laws and commands) and offer you eternal life. He wants to offer you salvation, which is to be saved by God from the consequences of sin. God will do all the work. All you must do is ask Him to save you. Right now, ask God to come into your life. Ask God to forgive you of your sins. Ask God to be your friend. If you did this and are sincere in your heart, I believe you are saved. Welcome into the family of our Lord and Savior Jesus Christ. Congratulations!

Before we can discover more steps to help with overcoming temptation, it is important to distinguish between an addiction, a stronghold, and a temptation. It may appear these three words are synonyms, with all three having the same meaning, but they are very different. Understanding these differences will help us move forward and identify if we are dealing with an addiction, a stronghold, or a temptation. I will cover what an addiction is and how to become free from an addiction, and I will cover what a stronghold is and how to become free from a stronghold. It is important we talk about addictions and strongholds, so we can see that temptation is very different and does not fall into either of these categories.

Let us talk about addictions first. It may shock you to know that only unsaved people (sinners) can have an addiction. Let us unpack this a bit. An addiction, in its simplest terms, is being unable to stop doing something that is hurting you. To put it more formally, Medical News Today states that, "Addiction is a psychological and physical inability to stop consuming a chemical, drug, activity, or substance, even though it is causing psychological and physical harm."[1] Only a sinner can have an addiction because they cannot stop consuming drugs, alcohol, pornography, tobacco, gambling, etc., even though it is causing them harm. How many times have you heard someone say, "I know smoking cigarettes is bad for me, but I can't stop smoking the darn things?" The cigarette is in control of the person. If the craving for that cigarette strikes, the person with the addiction will "light up" no matter what. People addicted to alcohol or drugs say they must have a drink or a "fix." A sinner cannot fix an addiction. You might ask, "Well, what about Alcoholics Anonymous or other rehab and treatment facilities that help people all the time?" I agree that Alcoholics Anonymous helps some people to stop drinking, but it does not and cannot offer them freedom from drinking. Alcoholics Anonymous says, "We understand now, that once a person has crossed the invisible line from heavy drinking to compulsive alcoholic drinking, they will always remain [an] alcoholic. So far as we know, there can be no turning back to 'normal' social drinking. 'Once an alcoholic—

---

[1] Medical News Today, October 26, 2018.

always an alcoholic' is a simple fact we have to live with."[2] This statement from Alcoholics Anonymous seems like bad news to me. I want to suggest to you the "gospel" or good news that those struggling with addiction can absolutely be free from the addiction. Alcoholics Anonymous takes the approach of people helping people, but I would suggest to you that someone with an addiction needs so much more than help from another person. They need to be made alive in Christ. They need the freedom only God can offer them. If you are a sinner and you have an addiction, there is only one solution to your problem. Salvation is the only cure for addiction. John 8:36 (NIV) says, *"So if the Son sets you free, you will be free indeed."* "The Son" is Jesus Christ, and if He sets you free, you will be free without a doubt. Jesus says in Luke 4:18-19, *"The Spirit of the Lord is upon me because he hath anointed me to preach the gospel to the poor; he hath sent me to heal the brokenhearted, to preach deliverance to the captives, and recovering of sight to the blind, to set at liberty them that are bruised."* Jesus wants to deliver and free the sinner. Jesus holds the key to unlock the handcuffs of addiction. The first and best step is to ask Jesus to save you and set you free! Once you are saved, it is so important to remember that your whole life has changed, and you are no longer the person you were before you were saved. You must believe 2 Corinthians 5:17 (NIV), which says, *"Therefore*

---

[2] 2020 CERES* e.V. Alcoholics Anonymous Continental European Region.

*if any man (or woman) be in Christ, he (or she) is a new creature:
old things are passed away; behold, all things become new."* God
has made us new creatures when He saved us. The old things
like addictions are no more. If you are saved, you cannot have an
addiction, because an addict is a slave to their addiction. They are
chained up by their addiction, and only God can truly free them.
God provides this freedom when He saved you.

I remember seeing a man be freed from addiction one Sunday
at our church. My grandfather was the pastor of the church I
attended growing up. My grandfather also had a day job working
at a local university. He had invited one of his friends, who also
worked at the university, to attend our church one Sunday. My
grandfather knew his good friend from work was unsaved. His
friend was also addicted to cigarettes, and he had a two-pack-
a-day cigarette habit. I had met my grandfather's friend before
when my grandfather would take me to work with him sometimes
during the summer. He was a nice man, and he always seemed
happy to see me. I was happy to see him on that Sunday my
grandfather had invited him to come to our church. I was about
ten years old and my grandfather had preached a really good
sermon that Sunday. After his sermon, he made an altar call and
asked if anyone wanted to give their life to Christ and be saved.
His friend leaped to his feet and ran down to the altar. He took
out a fresh pack of cigarettes from the inside of his jacket pocket

and threw them down hard to the floor, and he knelt at the altar. He wept, and my grandfather prayed for him, and the man asked God to save him and to come into his life. To this day, he testifies that on that day God not only saved him, but he also delivered him from an addiction to smoking cigarettes. He says that he went from a two-pack-a-day habit to not desiring to smoke a cigarette. He says that now he can barely stand the smell of a cigarette. Only God can provide this type of transformation.

Maybe your next question is: What about a person who had an addiction, and they get saved, but they continue to smoke, gamble, gossip, lie, etc.? Great question! That person has a stronghold and not an addiction. Before salvation, it was an addiction, but after salvation, it is a stronghold. You might think that this is just a simple case of semantics, but it is so much deeper than this. A stronghold, in the simplest terms, has a grip on your life, and you struggle to get free from it. Dr. Tony Evans adds, "A stronghold is a mindset that accepts a situation as unchangeable, even though we know it is against the will of God." An addiction has control over a person who cannot stop doing what their addiction is telling them to do, even though it is harming them. They cannot stop sinning and they are a slave to sin because ultimately sin rules their life, but Jesus offers freedom from sin. A person with a stronghold is free, but they may believe a lie that says they are not free. This lie is perpetuated by the person struggling with the stronghold.

Satan also lies to a person who has a stronghold, by telling them they will never be free from lusting or whatever stronghold is controlling them. The way to defeat a lie is to attack it with the truth. We find truth in God's Word—the Bible. John 8:32 (NIV) says, *"Then you will know the truth, and the truth will set you free."* We should always listen to God's viewpoint on everything, which is in the pages of the Bible, and it is the truth that we need to seek. Proverbs 3:5-6 (KJV) says, *"Trust in the Lord with all thine heart; and lean not unto thine own understanding. In all thy ways acknowledge him, and he shall direct thy paths."* If the stronghold lies and says you need to smoke marijuana, you need to attack that lie with the truth of God's Word. A stronghold is an area of sin that we allow to play a part in our lives, and we allow this stronghold to grab hold of us even though Christ, through our salvation, has set us free.

Many times, new Christians and even more mature Christians continue to struggle with bondage to strongholds because they do not understand or were not taught about the freedom from sin that their salvation has already provided for them. When I was saved at age thirteen, the assistant pastor of our church warned me about one lie the devil uses to trick new Christians. He told me, "The devil will tell you that you are not saved. He will try to convince you that you are the same and nothing about you has changed." This was great spiritual training because I questioned my salvation, wondered if I was really saved, and thought salvation was for older people and not a thirteen-year-old. I am so grateful for my assistant pastor's warning because when the temptation came to question my salvation, he had prepared me for the lies the devil would use. I pray that as the body of Christ, we will constantly and consistently expose the lies and tricks of the devil. We should tell new Christians that the devil will try to convince them that they are not saved. We should tell new Christians and all Christians that the devil will try to set up strongholds in their lives to keep them in bondage to something. It is important to remember that the devil cannot set up a stronghold in your life without your permission. Maybe you are thinking, I would never give the devil permission to set up a stronghold in my life. You give him this permission by accepting the lie he feeds you. Every lie the devil feeds you is an attempt to either set up a stronghold in you or to add to the stronghold he has already created. The devil wants to set up strongholds in your life because he wants a place in your mind he can retreat to and control your thoughts. For example, he feeds you a lie that you are not good enough, not educated enough, not pretty enough. Sadly, with your permission, because you have believed these lies, the devil establishes a stronghold or a place for him to gain access to your mind. He wants to create a habit in you where you repeatedly believe his lies and a place in your mind that he can access to keep you away from the Lord. Have you ever noticed how everything can go well and all it takes is for a certain thought to cross your mind to interrupt your peace? The devil enjoys using our past to disrupt our present. He will remind us of past failures and use them to trick us into believing we are still a failure.

"But thanks be to God! He gives us the victory through our Lord Jesus Christ. Therefore, my dear brothers and sisters, stand firm. Let nothing move you," 1 Corinthians 15:57-58 NIV. God has given us the victory through our Lord Jesus Christ, and we must use the truth of God's Word to defeat the lies of the devil and to destroy the walls of the strongholds we allowed him to create in our lives.

I wanted to cover the differences between addictions and strongholds because it will allow us to gain a more clear understanding of what temptation is and how we are to respond to it. We will also explore if it is possible to make our response to temptation automatic.

CHAPTER 3

Temptations Will Come, but How Will You Respond?

Chapter 2 discussed the first step to dealing with and overcoming temptation, with the first step being able to answer the question of if you belong to God. The next step to dealing with and overcoming temptation is to realize that temptation will come. If I were to walk up to you right now and warn you that, "Within the next thirty seconds, I am going to kick you in the leg," what would you do? Most likely, you would prepare some sort of defense. You might try a preemptive strike and try to kick me first. You might try to move your leg out of the way at the precise moment, so I miss kicking your leg. You might contact the police, tell them about my threat, and ask them to come to your aid. Most likely, you are prepared for my attack because you realize that if I kick you in the leg, it is probably going to hurt, and it may injure you. You realize that being kicked will not be a good thing. I warned you I was going to kick you and you took steps to prevent my attack. God's Word gives us a warning that temptation will come, and it is a common occurrence. Remember that 1 Corinthians 10:13 (NIV) says, *"No temptation has overtaken you except what is common to mankind."* With this prior knowledge, why do we allow the temptation to kick us around? If you and I are being honest, we give in to temptation more often than we would like to admit. The Apostle Paul writes in Romans 7:19 (NIV), *"For I do not do the good I want to do, but the evil I do not want to do—this I keep on doing."*

We realize that being tempted is not a sin. The Bible teaches us in Matthew 4:1-11, Mark 1:12-13, and Luke 4:1-13 that the Holy Spirit led Jesus to temptation by Satan. Jesus, who never sinned but faced temptation, is our proof that being tempted is not a sin. It is giving in to the temptation that is a sin. It is accepting the offer that the tempter or temptation promises that leads to sin. Every temptation is an offer you can either accept, reject, or defeat the temptation. These three choices offer different results.

Accepting the temptation or saying yes to the temptation leads to sin and is the worst choice a believer can make. When we accept and give in to temptation, we are making a choice that says, What I am being offered (because I have accepted it) is more appealing than what God offers me. God's offer is always what is best for you. However, if I can be honest for a minute, His offer does not always give us the instant gratification or pleasure we sometimes seek. Temptation begins in our minds. God offers, in the book of Isaiah 26:3 (KJV), to keep us in perfect peace. The Scripture says, *"Thou wilt keep him in perfect peace, whose mind is stayed on thee: because he trusteth in thee."* The danger of saying yes to temptation is that we forfeit the promise of God to keep us in perfect peace. Once we say yes to temptation, we are no longer keeping our minds stayed on God. When we say yes to temptation, we are saying no to God. Saying yes to temptation is blatantly rejecting the will of God for our lives, whether we realize it. The devil tempts us because he wants us to give in to the temptation, which is sinning, and therefore reject the "peace of God," so we will focus on what the temptation promises and not focus on and live out God's will for our lives.

It is easy to see that giving in to temptation and saying yes to temptation is not the right choice for a believer to make because it leads to sin, but what about saying no to temptation? This seems like the correct response a believer should make, right? "Just say no!" If the urge tempts you to curse out someone who has wronged you, just say no! If the urge temps you to cheat on your taxes, just say no! If you are a diabetic and your doctor has told you not to eat sugary foods, then just say no! to that piece of double chocolate cake that is winking at you. Does fighting temptation with the phrase, "Just say no" really work?

I remember being in school in the 1980s and being told to "Just say no" to drugs. "Just Say No" was an advertising campaign prevalent during the 1980s and early 1990s as a part of the U.S. "War on Drugs," aiming to discourage children from engaging in illegal recreational drug use by offering various ways of saying no. The slogan was created and championed by First Lady Nancy Reagan during her husband's presidency (Wikipedia)[3]. According to the *Chicago Tribune* newspaper, "A 2008 follow-up study funded by the National Institutes of Health found the campaign 'had no favorable effects on youth's behavior' and may have actually prompted some to experiment with drugs, an unintended 'boomerang' effect."[4] This anti-drug campaign, which had the support of the President of the United States and the backing of billions of taxpayers' dollars, did not work. I am not at all surprised that "Just say no" did not work, because illicit drug use is a symptom and an effect of a much deeper issue. People took illicit drugs back then and people continue to take and abuse illicit drugs now because this drug use directly ties to satanic and demonic activity that tempted and tricked people into trying drugs and getting high. If just saying no struggles to curb the appetite from wanting a piece of double chocolate cake, it will be

[3] Wikipedia, https://en.wikipedia.org/wiki/Recreational_drug_use.
[4] *Chicago Tribune*, "Fact Check: 'Just Say No' anti-drug campaigns have shown little success in past, October 27, 2017.

powerless to curb the appetite for illegal drugs, gluttony, cigarettes, envy, jealousy, and so many other sinful things that tempt us. Just saying no relies on willpower, grit, and self-determination.

Remember the book, The Little Engine That Could? It is the story of a long train that breaks down while carrying toys and treats for good little boys and girls. This long train was just about to go over a big hill when it broke down. As the story goes, the long train asks for help from other trains, large and small, that pass by, but they all refuse to help until a little blue steam engine helps. The little blue train hooks up to the long train filled with toys and treats. While it seems like an impossible task for the Little Engine, the little train uses willpower, grit, self-determination, and a clever catchphrase, "I think I can, I think I can, I think I can," and powers the long train over the hill. This is the phrase that the Little Engine kept repeating and the story suggests that the Little Engine's willpower, grit, self-determination, and clever catchphrase saved the day and what helped it to carry the long train over the big hill. This sounds good, and I believed every inch of this story when I was a child. As an adult, though, I realize *The Little Engine That Could* is only a fairy tale. Merriam-Webster defines a fairy tale as a made-up story (for children) that involves magical creatures or fantastic forces, where improbable events lead to a happy ending; a made-up story usually designed to mislead. If I told you to just say no to temptation or to rely on willpower, grit, or self-determination to fight temptation, I would be guilty of trying to get you to believe in a fairy tale. These tactics might work once or twice, but once your willpower runs out or once you are weak, you will give in to temptation if saying no or relying on your strength is all you have to work with. Remember that the devil does not waste time tempting you with something you dislike or you can easily resist. He tempts you with what you really like, and his goal is to get you to take the bait of the temptation, so you will not focus on God and instead focus on your fleshly desires. The Bible says in James 1:13-14 (NIV), *"When tempted, no one should say, "God is tempting me." For God cannot be tempted by evil, nor does he tempt anyone; but each person is tempted when they are dragged away by their own evil desire and enticed."*

The devil works to tempt you in the same way a fisherman might work to catch a fish. Fishing is one of my favorite hobbies. When I go fishing, I do not just show up at a lake or the ocean and start fishing. My most successful fishing trips involved planning. The day before the fishing trip is when I choose which body of water in which I want to fish. I also determine what type of fish I want to catch. Once I determine where I want to fish and the type of fish I most want to catch, I think about what types of bait I will use to lure the fish to bite. I do not waste my time using bait I know will not temp the fish to bite. I usually select a bait that has worked on other fish I have caught in the past. Once I arrive where the fish are, I will bait a sharp metal hook with the juiciest worm I can find. I use the worm to hide the sharp hook because I want the fish only to see and focus on that juicy and enticing worm and not to see the jagged, piercing hook attached to the worm. I drop the worm and the hook into the water, and I let it fall to the bottom. Sometimes, I get a fish to bite on the worm right away. Other times, I cleverly tug on the line and it makes the worm dance in front of the fish. I want to make sure the fish see, smell, touch, and eventually taste the meal I am offering them. I want to overload their senses so they cannot resist this juicy dancing worm. Chomp! The fish takes the bait and chomps down on the worm. Instead of enjoying the worm, the fish feels the intense pain of the sharp metal hook piercing its lip. This action alerts me I can now "set the hook."

Setting the hook means that once the fish has bitten the bait, I give my fishing rod a quick tug which fixes the barbed hook, so the fish cannot get away. Once I "set the hook," then it is time for me to reel the fish in. I want to take the fish out of the safety of the water and bring it to an unfamiliar environment, on land where I know it cannot breathe, swim, or fight. The devil's goal is to tempt and trick you and me, so he can carry us away from the safety of God's presence to an unfamiliar environment where we cannot fight against his weapons. Just as a fisherman selects an appropriate bait to catch a fish, the devil selects an appropriate temptation to tempt you. He wants to bait you into sinning by offering you something that appeals to your flesh. For example, he knows guys with big muscles or women with curves attract you, so he will dangle them in front of you, tempting you to look. He hopes you will do more than just look. Maybe you will fantasize about that person or undress them with your eyes.

In the Bible, the book of 2 Samuel 11 tells the story of King David who, from his palace, sees a beautiful woman bathing one evening. Struck by her beauty, David sends someone to find out about her. David's messenger reports back to him, so he now knows that her name is Bathsheba, and she is the wife of Uriah, a soldier in David's army, who is away fighting the Ammonites in Rabbah, a town in Judah. Even with this knowledge, David summons Bathsheba to his palace and he sleeps with her. Bathsheba returns home and later sends word to David that she is pregnant. Because he or his demons had studied David, the devil knows David will take the bait of a beautiful bathing woman, despite her being another man's wife. He used this bait to steal David's focus away from God and entice him to focus on his fleshly desires. We will talk more about this story later, but it was David's fleshly desires that caused him to sin because he took the bait the devil offered.

At other times, the enemy may use the bait of money, power, and success to tempt you to put everything, including God, on the back burner and move your selfish ambitions to the front. The enemy will help you climb the corporate ladder, provided your pursuit leads you to place money, power, and success ahead of almighty God. Money, power, and success are not bad things, but where we position these things in our lives can cause us to give them more importance than we give God. The enemy's goal is to get you to take the bait of whatever temptation he dangles in front of you so he can set the hook and use it to pull you away from God. If he can pull you away from God, he can control you. Being controlled by the enemy will lead to trouble, and many times, we do not even realize we have taken the bait.

My grandmother, who taught me how to fish when I was a young boy, used to have a poster she hung on a wall in her house. The poster was a picture of a fish with a hook in its mouth. The caption on the poster read: Even a fish won't get into trouble if it learns to keep its mouth shut. Is it possible to learn how to resist the enemy's temptations, so we do not take the bait and get hooked into doing things that are against the will of God? Sure, but first we need to discover that the enemy is not the only source of temptation. As much as I would like to blame everything on the enemy with temptation, the enemy is only one of three sources of temptation.

The second source of temptation for Christians are temptations that result from our own fleshly or evil desires. As we discussed earlier in James 1:14 (NIV), the Bible says, *"But each person is tempted when they are dragged away by their own evil desire and enticed."* So, a Christian can be dragged away by taking the bait the devil offers, and they can also be dragged away by their evil desires. The devil dangled the bait of Bathsheba in front of David, but because of his evil desires, David sends for Bathsheba and sleeps with her. Even with the forehand knowledge of knowing that Bathsheba is Uriah's wife. David lusts over Bathsheba, and he continues to sin by sleeping with Bathsheba. James 1: 15(KJV) says, *"Then when lust hath conceived, it bringeth forth sin: and sin, when it is finished, bringeth forth death."* James 1:14-15 shows the snowball effect of giving in to temptation. The story of David and Bathsheba proves and thoroughly illustrates the truth of this Scripture. David's sin of lust for Bathsheba brings forth the sin of adultery. When David finishes with Bathsheba, she returns home and later discovers she is pregnant. Because of the snowball effect of sin, David has an innocent husband and loyal soldier, Uriah, put to death to cover up his sin. Romans 6:23 (KJV) says, *"For the wages of sin is death; but the gift of God is eternal life through Jesus Christ our Lord."* David's sin cost Uriah his life. Giving in to our evil desires can have deadly consequences.

Giving in to the third source of temptation for a Christian can also have deadly consequences. This source involves temptations that come from our surrounding environment. The world is full of sinful influences and we have to resist the temptation to act, think, and function like the world. 1 John 2:15 (KJV) says, *"Love not the world, neither the things that are in the world. If any man love the world, the love of the Father is not in him."* The temptation to conform to what the world offers or what is popular in society bombards Christians daily. Television shows, movies, commercials, social media, and celebrities fight to tempt and influence us to take the bait of sinful offerings that directly oppose the teachings of the Bible—overrun us. For example, society stresses living your life the way you want to live it, doing whatever makes you happy, and defining yourself however you would like. It also puts a strong emphasis on relying on yourself and your abilities. Every day we face the temptation to live life on our terms. Every day we must decide if we will live according to the instructions God left for us in the Bible or allow what is popular in society to influence us. I like what Steve Arterburn, founder of New Life Ministries, has to say. "Seductive images are everywhere; subtle messages tell you it's okay to sin 'just a little,' and to make matters even worse, society doesn't just seem to endorse godlessness, it actually seems to reward it. Society spews forth a wide range of messages, all of which imply it is okay to rebel against God. These messages, of course, are extremely dangerous and completely untrue."

There is no room for grey areas with what God's instructions say and what society's opposing viewpoint suggests. As God's people, we must stand against any ideas, suggestions, or notions that are in contrast with the word of God which is the Bible. If we are not careful, society will influence us and tempt us to adopt a mindset where we think what God says in the Bible is wrong and what the popular rhetoric of our society says is right. As God's people, we must trust what God says and not society. Proverbs 14:12 (NIV) says, "*There is a way that appears to be right, but in the end, it leads to death.*" We cannot blindly trust that what our society may be subtly screaming at us is the right path to take or the correct way to think. Allowing society to light the pathway of ideas we walk on will lead to us being tempted to adopt and trust what society says and to reject what God says. Only what God says can we completely trust.

CHAPTER 4

God Wrote a Book, but I Am Too Busy To Read It!

G od wants us to trust Him. He wants to give us life, and He wants to be our Leader. He wants to guide us and has provided instructions for our daily lives in the Bible. He wrote down these instructions for us, but sadly a strong majority of us do not read the Bible very often. LifeWay Research conducted a survey and found that nearly seventy percent of churchgoing Christians do not read the Bible every day. How can this be? Is this true? Well, I can tell you it was the case for me.

For as long as I can remember, my family has always been devoted to the Lord. With my grandfather pastoring the church we attended, we were always in church, and I am very thankful for the foundation that growing up in a Christian home provided for me. When I was young, I would see my grandmother reading and studying the Bible. She would sit at her dining room table with multiple Bibles, dictionaries, and concordances, diligently reading and studying. She was not studying because she attended Bible College and had a test coming up or she had a class to teach or some other obligation. She was studying because she loved the Lord and wanted to connect with God and get to know Him better by reading His Word.

I never read the Bible very much. Growing up, the only Scripture I memorized was John 11:35, *"Jesus wept."* I only memorized this verse, because my Sunday school teacher told us one week that the following week each student had to come to class, having memorized a verse of Scripture. Of course, I picked the shortest verse in the Bible, "Jesus wept," and this was my memory verse. I had no idea why Jesus wept. I did not bother to learn what made Jesus cry. I had to memorize a verse, and this two-word verse was right up my alley. I attended church every Sunday, and I attended Sunday School, but reading the Bible was the last thing on my mind. I did not read the Bible when I was young, and I did not read the Bible when I got older. To be completely honest, I didn't start reading the Bible daily until twelve or thirteen years ago. I am almost embarrassed to admit that, but it is the truth. I was not reading the Bible, the word of God. I was saved, and I was coming to church regularly.

Fifteen years ago, my wife and I joined a new church. It was the first church I had joined outside of the church my grandfather pastored. I even brought a brand-new Bible. It was a nice leather-bound parallel Bible. A parallel Bible shows multiple versions of the Bible side-by-side for comparison. I brought this Bible because the pastor at our new church would preach and teach from both the King James Version and New International Version. When he would preach and teach, I would break out my new Bible and follow along. If you looked at me following along with my pastor, I could fool you into thinking I picked up my Bible on more than just Sunday mornings. I looked like a Christian who reads the Bible every day. Wearing a nice suit and tie, I would carry my Bible to church. I looked the part. If you were casting actors for a play that had a church scene and you had a part for a good-looking man wearing a suit and tie and holding the Bible, I would have gotten that part. For the first three years of us attending our new church, I played the part of a well-dressed Christian man, who owned a Bible and carried it to church every Sunday. My reality? I never opened it outside of the church. I kept my Bible in the back window of the car. The Bible was a prop I used while playing my part as a "good" Christian.

I remember looking the part this one Sunday. When it was time for my pastor to preach the word of God and he said for us to turn our Bibles to a verse of Scripture, like a "good" Christian, I stood up and turned to the Scripture my pastor was going to be preaching about. It was at that moment that I heard God speak to me. He said, "Aswin, this is the first time that you have opened your Bible all weeklong. The last time you opened your Bible was the week before, at this same time at church on Sunday morning when your pastor asked the congregation to open your Bibles." Except for a few minutes on a Sunday morning, I was not reading the Bible at all. Right away, I received a conviction, and I asked God to forgive me. I made a promise to God that I would read my Bible every day.

I kept my promise and read my word each day. It was tough at first. I had to force myself to read the Bible, but I promised God. Reading God's Word daily, I discovered my life was changing. I was getting to know God, learning more about Jesus, and learning more about myself. Through reading the Bible daily, God made changes in my life. I joined a ministry at our church. By this time, I had been a member of our church for several years, content with sitting on the sidelines doing nothing. Reading the Bible every day and getting to know more about God compelled me to get off the sidelines and become active in ministry and an active member of our church.

Reading the Bible every day was influencing everything about me. I was becoming better. I was becoming a better husband because I was reading Scriptures like 1 Peter 3:7 and Ephesians 5:25-33. I was learning what it truly means to be a godly husband. I was learning how to love my wife like Christ loved the church with unconditional love. I was also becoming a better father because I was reading about the role of a father in the Bible. Ephesians 6:4 was helping to shape me. I was learning that God requires me to play an active role in the spiritual nurturing my son needs. I was learning that being a good father was about more than throwing the football around with my son or watching him play the drums at his band concert at school. Being a good father was about teaching him about God and leading him to establish a relationship of his own with Jesus Christ. Reading the Bible every day was also changing the type of friend I was to my buddies. Instead of always talking about sports or work, I talk about the Lord. God led me to witness to some of my friends to lead them to Christ. As God would lead me, I would buy them a Bible and encourage them to read, call, or text me if they had any questions, so we could find the answers together. At my church, I teach classes that focus on the Bible as it relates to discipleship. It is amazing to me that I am teaching classes about the very book, that at one time, I was not even reading before. Look at God! Now, I am telling my story and writing this book.

This book is based on the word of God. I am only able to write this book because God spoke to me one Sunday morning and let me see that just owning and carrying a Bible was not enough. I needed to open my Bible and read it every day. God is amazing. God has changed my life through the reading and hearing of His

Word. My faith in God has grown and my faith in His ability to provide for everything I need in my life has grown. Romans 10:17 (KJV) says, *"Faith comes by hearing and hearing by the word of God."*

Reading the Bible every day is essential for the spiritual growth and development of every Christian. If you are not reading the Bible every day, please start to do so from now on. Make yesterday the last day you did not read the Bible.

I want to help you with this. God allowed me to see that I must see the Word of God as spiritual food or as daily bread. We are all taught how important good nutrition is for our bodies. The spiritual food of the word of God is immeasurably more important for you. Never fast from the daily bread that is the word of God! Also, it is important not to give yourself any excuses not to read the Bible. When I first started reading the Bible, I had to force myself to get up a little earlier each morning. I knew I would never "find the time" to read my Bible, so I had to make time to read on purpose. You must make time to read your Bible because other things will always vie for your attention. You know, we can make time to check our cell phones after every beep, chime, ring, ding, and alert. We can make time to eat at least three meals a day. We can make time to drive in traffic on our way to work and we can work all day long, and even make time to work overtime. We can then leave work and drive in traffic all over again. We can make time to stop by the cleaners and pick up the dry-cleaning. Then we can make time to rush to our homes, pick up the kids, and take them to basketball practice or dance practice. Then we can come back home and park ourselves in front of the television and binge watch something on Netflix or Hulu. Then we can make time to pick up the phone to call our buddies or our girlfriends and talk about this and that. If we can make time for all these things every day, why can we not make time to read the life-changing, life-sustaining, word of God? I like what Sheri Bell wrote in an article I read online. She said, "When we forgo reading the Bible, what we are really saying to God is that we are too busy to put in the work of really knowing Him. That we are good with having a distant relationship with Him. That we sure are happy that He's just a prayer away—but please don't ask us to read 'that boring, irrelevant book.'"[5] A "boring, irrelevant book." Sheri Bell's words are hard to swallow as she describes the attitude many Christians have toward the Bible. She must be right because an overwhelming majority of churchgoing Christians do not read the Bible every day. There is a present danger in being biblically illiterate. Even the Bible says we should read the Bible. 1 Timothy 4:13 (NIV) says, *"Until I come, devote yourself to the public reading of Scripture, to preaching and to teaching."* Also, Matthew 4:4 (KJV) says, *"But he answered and said, It is written, Man shall not live by bread*

---

[5]Sheri Bell, October 4, 2018, "5 Reasons Christians Must Read the Bible."

alone, but by every word that proceedeth out of the mouth of God.” Additionally, Psalms 119:105 (NIV) says, *“Your word is a lamp for my feet, a light on my path.”*

Sadly, many Christians are walking without a lamp on a path covered in darkness. That is a surefire way to trip and fall! God, through His Word, wants to light your path and show you the way, but you must use His light. You must read your Bible every day. Encouraging you to read your Bible every day is one of the major goals of this book.

CHAPTER 5

The Bible is a Powerful Weapon

Another major goal of this book is that we learn to use God's Word as a weapon. We need to use this weapon to fight against attacks from Satan and to strike against the lies he uses to create a stronghold in us. We also need to use God's Word as a weapon to attack temptation.

The word of God is alive and active. This is an incredible blessing for the body of Christ. Thank you, Jesus! I love that God's Word is not dead and doing nothing, but it is ALIVE and ACTIVE. Ephesians 6:17 (KJV) says, *"And take the helmet of salvation and the sword of the spirit, which is the word of God."* Hebrews 4:12 (NIV) also describes the word of God as a weapon. It says, "For the word of God is alive and active. Sharper than any double-edged sword, it penetrates even to dividing soul and spirit and marrow, it judges the thought and attitudes of the heart."

A sword is a weapon used to fight an enemy, right? Our enemies are Satan and sin, and if we are not reading and using the word of God, we are on a battlefield without a sword. Let me say that again. If we are not reading, using, and applying the word of God, we are on a battlefield without a sword—without a weapon. That sounds dangerous!

The word of God is so powerful and so vital to the life of a Christian that Satan does not want us to read and will throw everything he can in our paths to distract us from reading. The word of God is so powerful that when Jesus was led up into the wilderness to be tempted by Satan, he tried to use the word of God to tempt Jesus. Can you believe that Satan tried to use Scripture to tempt Jesus? Well, yes, Satan tried to use Scripture to trick and tempt Jesus. In Satan's second temptation found in Matthew 4:6 (KJV), Satan is talking, and he says, *"If thou be the Son of God, cast thyself down: for it is written, He shall give his angels charge concerning thee: and in their hands they shall bear thee up, lest at any time thou dash thy foot against a stone."* Satan was trying to quote Psalms 91:11-12 (KJV) that says, *"For he shall give his angels charge over thee, to keep thee in all thy ways. They shall bear thee up in their hands, lest thou dash thy foot against a stone."* So, Satan is using the word of God to try to trick and tempt Jesus. If you compare what Satan says with the actual Scripture, he was trying to quote from the book of Psalms, but he leaves out part of the

Scripture. Satan will always try to twist God's Word. Basically, Satan says to Jesus, "If you are really the Son of God, then prove it to the religious groups like the Pharisees and Sadducees who will become your toughest critiques. Cast yourself down and let them see the angels rush to your rescue and lift you up. Then they will believe you are the Son of God." Even though he misquoted the Scripture, Satan knows the Bible, and he recognizes that the Bible is powerful and true. He recognizes that what is in the Bible is vital to the life of a believer, and that is why he does not want you to read the Bible. He will fight and employ demons and use people to do everything they can to get you to not read your Bible. He will tell your boss to give you extra work and force overtime, so you spend your time concentrating on work and not reading the Bible. When it is time to read the Bible, he will cause your kids to need you more than ever. When it is time to read the Bible, he will try to make your cell phone ring with people who have the juiciest gossip to share. He will cause people to ring your doorbell, trying to sell you stuff you do not need. He will do anything to distract you and keep you from reading the word of God. Satan knows that the Bible is our power to resist him and his attacks. If he can get us not to read the Bible, he can take away from us the sword that God has given us to defeat him and temptations. This is Satan's preemptive strike against the body of Christ. The Free Dictionary by Farlex says that a preemptive strike is a surprise attack launched to prevent the enemy from doing it to you.

Satan tried a preemptive strike against Jesus when he was born. He convinced King Herod to become jealous of the baby Jesus. Satan knew that if he could get King Herod to feel a threat to his position as king, that jealousy would drive him to murder. Herod ordered the death of every male child age two and under. An angel spoke to Joseph, Jesus's earthly father, and told him to get up and escape to Egypt because Herod was searching for baby Jesus to kill him. Of course, this preemptive strike by Satan did not work, but if he will launch a surprise attack against Jesus, he will try to launch attacks against you.

Notice that the devil tries to attack Jesus when he is born and when he feels Jesus is vulnerable. The devil launches these same types of attacks against us when we are born again. He tries to convince new Christians they are not saved. He tries to convince new Christians that nothing about them has changed. He wants them to believe they are still the same as they were before God saved them. He does this because the devil does not want you to know what your new identity in Christ means. He does not want you to discover how to use the Bible as a weapon. The Bible is a weapon the devil cannot resist or fight against. His best defense is to do everything he can to keep you from reading the Bible. If you do not read the Bible, you allow the devil to strip the sword of the Spirit right out of your hands. You cannot defeat temptation and live a life that is pleasing to God unless you devote yourself to reading the Bible daily. God wrote the Bible and it is required reading for anyone who considers themselves a child of God. It is also required reading if you are going to defeat temptation.

Have you ever imagined what life could be like now if Adam and Eve had defeated temptation in the Garden of Eden? For a long time, I had been angry with Adam and Eve. I wanted to ask them, "Why did you eat the fruit? Do you know the harm that you're giving in to temptation has cost all of humanity?" I wanted to ask them these burning questions and many more. I also wondered why God prominently placed the Tree of Knowledge of Good and Evil in the middle of the garden. Why didn't God place the tree on the outskirts of the Garden of Eden, so it would not tempt Adam and Eve? I now realize God did not create Adam and Eve as robots. He allowed them to have the choice to obey His command or not to obey His command. For a while, Adam and Eve wisely obeyed God's instructions, even though the tree was prominently placed in the middle of the garden. They obeyed God because following God's instructions was more important than eating a piece of fruit. At least that was the case until a crafty serpent tempted them to disobey God and make a piece of fruit more important than God's command. We know that Satan somehow entered the serpent, so he could intentionally use the serpent to deceive Eve. Revelation 12:9 lets us know that it was Satan as a serpent who deceived Eve when it says, "And the great dragon was cast out, that old serpent called the Devil, and Satan, which deceiveth the whole world: he was cast out into the earth, and his angels were cast out with him." Let us look closely at Genesis 3 1-11 (NIV). It says, *"Now the serpent was more crafty than any of the wild animals the Lord God had made. He said to the woman, "Did God really say, 'You must not eat from any tree in the garden'?"*

²The woman said to the serpent, "We may eat fruit from the trees in the garden, ³but God did say, 'You must not eat fruit from the tree that is in the middle of the garden, and you must not touch it, or you will die.'"

⁴"You will not certainly die," the serpent said to the woman.

⁵"For God knows that when you eat from it your eyes will be opened, and you will be like God, knowing good and evil."

⁶When the woman saw that the fruit of the tree was good for food and pleasing to the eye, and also desirable for gaining wisdom, she took some and ate it. She also gave some to her husband, who was with her, and he ate it.

⁷Then the eyes of both of them were opened, and they realized they were naked; so they sewed fig leaves together and made coverings for themselves.

⁸Then the man and his wife heard the sound of the Lord God as he was walking in the garden in the cool of the day, and they hid from the Lord God among the trees of the garden.

⁹*But the Lord God called to the man, "Where are you?"*

¹⁰*He answered, "I heard you in the garden, and I was afraid because I was naked; so I hid."*

¹¹*And he said, "Who told you that you were naked? Have you eaten from the tree that I commanded you not to eat from?"*

Notice Satan's first question, using the serpent, was a question about God's Word. God's word is what Satan fears and God's Word is what Satan is powerless against, unless he can keep you from reading God's Word or if he can twist your understanding of God's Word. He asks Eve, "Did God really say, 'You must not eat from any tree in the garden?'" Genesis 3:1 (KJV). Satan twists God's Words and he asks Eve a question about what God had said to Adam and Eve. What God said was that they could eat from every tree in the garden, except the tree in the middle of the garden. It is so important we know and understand clearly what God's Word says because Satan will always try to twist God's Word and use it to deceive us. In verse four, Satan blatantly lies to Eve. Satan says, "You will not certainly die." Satan lies to Eve because he wants her to believe that disobeying God does not have consequences. Satan always lies. John 8:44 says that Satan is the father of lies. Lying is one of Satan's top strategies. He will tell you all about the pleasures of sin but will lie or leave out the consequences of sin. If we are going to defeat Satan's lies, we must fill our minds with the truth of God's Word so we can recognize Satan's lies.

According to Adherents,[6] there are some 4,300 religions in the world. The devil is perfectly fine with you practicing any one of the other 4,299 religions. But if you choose to follow Christ, he will do everything he can to twist God's Word to deceive you. I wish Eve had not taken the bait and had not even responded to the devil. Every time the serpent tried to talk to her, I wish Eve had repeated what God had already told her and Adam in Genesis 3:2, *"You must not eat fruit from the tree that is in the middle of the garden, and you must not touch it, or you will die."* I wish Adam and Eve knew they needed to focus on what God said and ignore what the devil said. They needed to run away from the devil and run to God. James 4:7 (KJV) says, *"Submit yourselves therefore to God. Resist the devil, and he will flee from you."* I wish they knew how to defeat this temptation. How different their lives could have been if they had listened to Almighty God who made and created them, instead of listening to the devil disguised as a serpent who only wanted to deceive them. How can I be upset with Adam and Eve, though, when I, too, have listened to the devil's lies and have sinned and given in to temptation? I am grateful that now I see the story of Adam and Eve as a warning of what can happen when I take my focus off God and give in to temptation.

---

[6]Adherents is an independent, non-religiously affiliated organization that monitors the number and size of the world's religions.

The story of Adam and Eve is also a lesson on the dangers of getting too comfortable with a serpent also known as a snake. The devil uses a snake to disguise himself from Adam and Eve. He uses a snake because the nature of a snake most closely resembles the nature of the devil. Snakes are crafty ambush predators. They will sit and wait with great patience until the precise moment and then they strike, viciously attacking their prey with razor-sharp teeth and fangs. The enemy viciously attacks Adam and Eve and tricks them into disobeying God. The attack is vicious because the devil knew that tricking them into sinning would have great and grave consequences. He knew that his sin of pride and his sin of wanting to be God was what got him kicked out of heaven. He wanted Adam and Eve to follow his plan and disobey God. Disobeying God is at the root of every sin. If you tell a lie, you have disobeyed God's command that says, "Thou shall not lie." If you are worried about money or a health diagnosis, you are disobeying God's Word in Philippians 4:6 that says, "Be anxious for nothing."

After Eve's conversation with the snake, she was so anxious to try the fruit that she and Adam blatantly disobeyed God's directions. They disobey God because they had gotten too comfortable with a talking snake. The Bible does not tell us, but I believe this was not the first time the devil had disguised himself as a snake to talk to Adam and Eve. How else could it be explained that Eve was not surprised that a snake was talking to her? She was not alarmed by the snake's presence at all. A talking snake raised no suspicions or questions for Adam and Eve. Eve talked to the snake and Adam did not raise one objection. Adam and Eve had become comfortable with the devil disguised as a snake. In Genesis 3, Adam and Eve did not find it strange that a snake talked to them. Adam, who God had given authority and a responsibility to name the animals, did not find it strange that the snake knew more about God than they did. More alarming than a talking snake was a snake questioning the word of Almighty God. They made the mistake of getting comfortable and trusting this snake disguised as the devil, whose mission was to trick and trip God's people into craving the pleasures of sin. Adam and Eve removed their focus from the instructions God had given them concerning the tree and its fruit and, instead, focused on why eating the fruit might benefit them. A temptation will take your focus away from what God has said. A temptation will work to minimize what God has said, intending to maximize your focus on what the temptation can offer.

The book of Job is the picture of a man who kept his focus on God. Unlike Adam and Eve, Job teaches us a way that we can win against temptation. We can win against temptation by eschewing evil. Eschew means to avoid something on purpose. Job deliberately and intentionally avoided evil. To rise to the level of eschewing, something requires avoidance. For example, if you decided you were going to eschew walking in puddles of water after it has rained. Simply walking around a puddle of water when you saw one would not rise to the level of eschewing puddles of water. If you practiced eschewing puddles of water, you would deliberately refuse to walk down a street with a puddle of water. If you practiced eschewing puddles of water, you would not even go outside on a cloudy day or go outside after it had rained because you would know that puddles of water would be everywhere. Eschewing puddles of water means you deliberately avoid going anywhere there might be the slightest chance that a puddle of water might be. Eschewing evil requires the work of dedicating our lives completely to God. Our focus must remain on God, even when Satan and his temptations work to distract us.

CHAPTER 6

Attend a Seminar, Create a Habit, Write a Code, Defeat Temptation

Okay, I have a question for you. When was the last time you had to tell your liver to function or tell your gallbladder to make bile and use this bile to break down fat? When was the last time you had to tell your pancreas to secrete enzymes to help with digestion or tell your pancreas to help your body regulate your blood sugar? When was the last time you had to tell your heart to beat and pump blood throughout your body? The answer is that you do not have to tell your body to do these things, because our bodies do these things automatically. Our bodies perform these functions automatically without us having to flip on a switch or even having to think about it. I am sure you have never heard someone say, "Oh, my goodness, I forgot to tell my small intestine to pass that waste on to my large intestine. I keep forgetting to do that." You have never heard someone say that because thank God, it happens automatically. It happens automatically! When your body needs to process food or pump blood or when your brain needs to tell your eyes to blink, it does it automatically without your thinking about it.

Wouldn't it be great that when temptations come our way, just as our heart automatically beats and pumps blood, we could automatically resist temptation? Wouldn't it be awesome if we never have to worry and struggle with temptation, because we are automatically programmed or hardwired to resist temptation?

We probably think it would be great to be automatically made by God to resist temptation but wouldn't that just make us a robot? If God wanted a robot, He certainly could have created one. Instead, He created us with the ability to make choices. We can choose to follow Him, or we can choose to follow a path that will lead us to give in to temptation and end with us sinning. God has saved us, and He wants us to grow in our relationship with Him to a place where we ultimately choose Him, even though we may be tempted to choose something else. God does not tempt us, but He allows temptation so we can grow in our relationship with him and see that He is more to be desired than whatever temptation is calling out to us. The Bible says, *"When tempted, no one should say, 'God is tempting me,'"* James 1:13 (NIV). When we are tempted, our temptation requires a response. As I mentioned before, our response to temptation will be to say yes or no, or we can choose to defeat the temptation. Saying yes leads to sin. Saying no is only a temporary fix that relies on our willpower, grit, and self-determination that will eventually fail. Defeating the temptation is the only solution. To defeat temptation, we must submit to God. Submitting to God will cause us to resist the tempter or temptation.

We have established that when we are tempted, our temptation requires a response. We have also established that our best response to temptation is a response that defeats the temptation. Is it possible to make this response that defeats temptation happen as automatically as a heartbeat? Maybe.

On August 22, 2013, I was required to attend a work seminar in Falls Church, Virginia. It was not unusual for me to attend a seminar or training, but I found the timing to be a little puzzling. Just two weeks before this seminar, I had surgery to fix a torn Achilles tendon, one of the worst sports injuries imaginable. I had injured myself playing basketball with my brother. I remember driving hard into the basketball lane ready to embarrass my brother and show him that I could still dominate him on the basketball court. Before I could put up the shot toward the basket, I heard a pop, or at least I thought I heard a popping sound. It turned out that my Achilles tendon had ruptured. I have played sports all my life and I have gone through my share of injuries, but this was different. My other injuries usually required a cast or a brace and some rest. Usually, within a couple of weeks, I was back on the field or on the court. This injury was different because my doctor said that I needed more than a cast and some rest. I needed surgery to repair my Achilles. He also said I would require several weeks of physical therapy to help regain strength in my foot and to rebuild my calf muscle.

I was a bit worried about the kind of response that I might receive from my employer, when they found out that I had an injury that required surgery and required that I would miss some time from work. To my surprise, my employer had been so sympathetic and understanding when I first injured myself. I was amazed that one of the vice presidents, who was my immediate supervisor, said not to worry about rushing back to the office. He told me to take a week off and then I could continue to recover and work from home. Wow! I could work from home. I took a week off and I was glad I did. Following the surgery, I was in a great deal of pain. By the next week, thankfully, the pain had subsided. So, I grabbed my crutches and hopped into my home office. I set up my laptop, logged into my work system, and was ready to take my first work phone call from home. Within five minutes of signing into my work system, my cell phone rang. It was my supervisor. After he asked me a few questions about how my surgery went, he asked if I was still taking pain medicine. I told him I had been taking some medicine for the first few days after my surgery, but now I felt like I no longer needed it.

With much enthusiasm, he said, "Oh, that's great, Aswin! Since you are not taking any pain medicine and since you injured your left foot and not your right foot, I want you to drive out to Virginia next week for a seminar."

"What!" was what I wanted to scream at him. Was he kidding me? I had just the scariest injury of my life and he wanted me to drive to another state to attend a stupid work seminar!

I did not want to go, because I thought it was just going to be another boring seminar. I also was not sure how I would handle getting in and out of the car and how different driving might be while I was still wearing a cast, even though it was on my left foot. With my doctor's approval and the aid of crutches and a knee roller, begrudgingly, I went to the seminar.

I must admit that it felt good to be behind the wheel driving again. My wife had been driving me to my doctor's appointments and to the local pharmacy to get my prescriptions. She had worked so hard taking care of me, and taking care of our son, Aswin Jr., who was eight years old then. At least my being out of the house, attending this seminar would give her a break for the day from one of her two Aswins. I was enjoying driving again, I just wished I was controlling the destination. Attending a work seminar was not my idea. The crazy thing was that it ended up being easily the best work seminar I had ever attended. The Bible says in Romans 8:28 (KJV), *"And we know that all things work together for good to them that love God, to them who are the called according to his purpose."* God was working things together for my good, and I did not even realize it then.

A man named Robb Best taught the seminar and it was a seminar on the brain and how we could use brain science to do our jobs better and make more money. It was a great seminar that inspired my colleagues to use this information to increase their work productivity and make more money. It inspired me to learn more about our brains and how our minds communicate with God. After all, it was God who made our brains. One thing I remember from the class is that scientists only understand about ten percent of how our brains work. Scientists estimate not understanding ninety percent of how the brain functions. It immediately hit me that ninety percent of how the brain works, which scientists do not understand, must be reserved for God. I believe God allows us to use the ten percent of the brain that the scientific community is aware of, to carry out everyday tasks and functions. I also believe the other ninety percent of the brain the scientific community does not understand is reserved for us through faith to discover who God is and why He must be the central figure of our lives.

When was the last time you were able to figure God out? When was the last time you guessed how God was going to fix one of your problems by thinking real hard, using your intellect and rationality? Then, because you are so smart, God solved your problem exactly the way you thought He would. If God worked this way, it would say more about your intelligence and rationale than God's ability to solve problems. Many times, the method God uses to bring you out of a situation will remain a mystery to you and sometimes you do not quite understand why God allows certain things to happen in your life. How many times have the pressures of life almost made you want to throw in the towel, but you did not give up and God made a way? God will do things in your life that you may not understand, but He gives us the faith to trust Him.

In the Bible, Job, through really difficult situations around him like the death of his children and losing all his livestock, suggested in his own words that God was trying to slay him, but his brain said, "Yet will I trust Him." Job felt God was killing him, but he still trusted God, anyway. Ask Abraham in the Bible what he was thinking when God said to go to a mountain in the region of Moriah and sacrifice his long-awaited son, Isaac, as a burnt offering. Both men had to be using that ninety-percent of the brain that scientists do not yet understand because trusting God, when you feel like He is slaying you and He has told you to sacrifice your son, cannot be explained by the ten percent of the brain that the scientists are familiar with. It can only be explained by that ninety percent I believe is reserved for God.

I want you to think about your life. Have you seen God make a way out of no way? Have you seen God keep you safe from impending danger? Have you seen God turn situations around and change people and circumstances to open doors that were previously shut? I bet you have a testimony about something in your life that only God can get the credit for bringing you out of. Job and Abraham certainly have a testimony about God's abundant blessings. At the end of their stories, these men were so richly blessed because God allowed them to use that ninety percent of their brains scientists do not understand. God allowed both men to trust and obey him at pivotal moments in their lives.

God uses pivotal moments in your life to draw you closer to Him. He has created us with the goal of us getting to know Him better. He wants to connect us to His Word, the Bible, and He wants us to adopt His frame of reference, mindset, and His perspective on everything.

Researchers at the University of Oxford wanted to find out if our brains are wired for God. They did a massive number of experiments using people from all over the world who had different cultural backgrounds and experiences. They were trying to uncover if there is a "God spot" in our brains. Is there a spot in our brains that is responsible for our belief in God? They concluded that there is no such spot. Mike McHargue says, "God doesn't simply move into a spot in our brains—God redecorates."[7] Our brains are ultimately reserved for God and to connect with God and connect with the truth of God. Getting to know God intimately requires that God "redecorate" our brains and that God moves into those places in our minds He has reserved for us to connect intimately with Him. I believe during our process of salvation that God moves into our minds, and He allows us to get to know Him by allowing us to access parts of our minds that have always been reserved for Him. I know sometimes it feels like we chose God, and we gave God access to our minds and hearts. The truth is, God chooses us, and He has given you access to parts of your brain/mind that were off-limits to you before your process of salvation. John 15:16 (NIV)says, *"You did not choose me, but I chose you and appointed you so that you might go and bear fruit— fruit that will last—and so that whatever you ask in my name the Father will give you."* God is in control of our lives and He gives us access to parts of our minds that are not found in brain science literature. He opens your understanding because He wants to use you to produce good works or as John 15:16 says to "bear fruit." This new access that God gives us to our minds allows us to trust God like Job, even when our circumstances make us feel like He is slaying us. God's unique ability to give us peace in the middle of

---

[7] *Relevant Magazine.* "How Your Brain is Wired for God." July 1, 2014.

a storm is proof of His love for us, and it demonstrates that He is in control. Many times, when we should panic, we remain calm. When we should cry, God fills us with joy.

I wanted to cry with excitement at what God was showing me at the work seminar that I did not want to attend. I was particularly interested in learning how habits are formed. According to Wikipedia, "a habit is a routine of behavior that is repeated regularly and occurs unconsciously. Habit formation is the process by which a behavior, through regular repetition, becomes automatic or habitual." According to science, it takes twenty-one days for us to do something each day for those twenty-one days for it to form a habit. So, for twenty-one days, if you decide you are going to do ten push-ups when you wake up, you will need to do this for twenty-one straight days before your brain will remind you when you wake up to do push-ups. It is like your brain talks and says to you, "Okay, you woke up. Now, remember to do ten push-ups." Science further says it takes sixty-three days of us doing the same thing each day, like ten push-ups, for our brains to write a code about this habit. Now we can think of writing code as what a computer programmer does to a computer. They write a code, and now the computer must perform a certain operation every time at a certain point. For example, when your computer starts up and you see the Apple logo or Dell logo, some computer programmer wrote a code and now the computer must perform the code that the programmer wrote. So, to go back to our push-up example, after your twenty-one days of doing push-ups, it becomes a habit, but after sixty-three days of doing push-ups, your brain writes a code and says this is what we do. It no longer needs to remind you as it did before. Before, your brain would kind of talk to you and would say, "Hey, buddy, you do ten push-ups in the morning, when you wake up." Now when you wake up you automatically do push-ups and your brain does not even need to remind you. As children, our parents told us to brush our teeth every day. At first, they had to make us brush our teeth, but over time, we formed a habit of brushing our teeth when we wake up in the morning. As time passed, our brains wrote a code that said when we wake up, we brush our teeth. Question? This week, how many times did you leave the house for work or school and forget to brush your teeth? My guess would be zero times, because your brain first formed a habit, then wrote a code about this habit, and now you brush your teeth automatically before you leave the house. As you formed that habit, you can reverse it by intentionally not brushing your teeth for twenty-one days. After sixty-three days of not brushing your teeth, your brain will write code that says when you wake up you no longer brush your teeth, but I do not suggest you break this habit or unwrite this code.

Habit formation and brain coding were some of the information that I was most fascinated by when I left the work seminar. I took detailed notes because I felt God sent me to this seminar and wanted me to use some of this information for other purposes that He would soon reveal. The Lord stirred up thoughts and ideas inside of me that confirmed why I had to attend the seminar. It was not to better perform for my employer and make the company more money. This knowledge was to be used to grow closer to God and to be a blessing to God's people. The Lord showed me how to use the science of habit formation and brain codes to help us deal with the very real danger of yielding to temptation. Now before you get mad at me and say, "Okay, is he going to try to tell us to use science to solve a spiritual problem of yielding to temptation?" I would remind you that God created science and our brains. Genesis 1:1(KJV) says, *"In the beginning, God created the heavens and the earth."* That was astronomy and earth science and God created them. Genesis 2:7 (KJV) says, *"And the Lord God formed man of the dust of the ground and breathed into his nostrils the breath of life; and man became a living soul."* 1 Corinthians 15:46 (NIV) says, *"The spiritual did not come first, but the natural, and after that the spiritual."* I would also remind you that God is sovereign, and He can use anything or anyone to accomplish His purposes. I am so grateful He is using me to help others to defeat temptation.

One of the biggest keys to defeating temptation is to fill yourself with the truth of God's Word that is found in the Bible.

I want to encourage you to form a habit of reading the Bible every day. Remember the devil is our enemy who does not want us to read the Bible. Sadly, many of us, according to statistics, are allowing the devil to defeat us in this area. This is a strategic attack by the devil because he knows that the Bible contains the truth that will expose the lies he feeds us. We need the truth of God's Word to defeat the lies of the enemy. I want to push you to start a new habit today and begin reading the Bible daily. Just try reading the Bible for twenty-one straight days. Do not worry about reading a certain number of pages or chapters per day. Just read whatever you can. When I first started reading the Bible daily, I started reading a few Scriptures each day. I was reading the Bible every day out of obedience to God and this caused a new hunger to rise in me to get to know God in a more personal way. I want you to pray and ask God to help you to commit to reading the Bible every day. Ask God to open your understanding about His Word and ask Him to create a hunger for His Word inside of you. This is an important prayer I would like for you to pray. I believe if you will ask God these things, He will answer your prayer and He will give you a hunger for His Word. After you read the Bible for twenty-one straight days, you will have created a habit of reading the Bible daily. I urge you to continue past the twenty-one days and reach sixty-three consecutive days of reading the Bible so your brain will write the code we talked about before. For me, reading the Bible every day is now automatic. I cannot function normally without reading the Bible. Even when my schedule gets busy, something forces me to make time to read God's Word. I like to read in the morning and before I do anything else, I grab my Bible to read and I also use this time to pray. Now I must admit that in the beginning, when I was first tried to make daily Bible reading a habit, it was a lot of work. I know this sounds bad, but I had to force myself to read the word of God. I had to force myself to intentionally take the time to read the book that God wrote. Amazingly, though, after some days passed, I began to really enjoy my daily reading. I knew I was doing something that had benefits for my soul!

The devil does not want you to read your Bible, because he knows that God's Word is a powerful weapon of warfare against him. He realizes that if you read your Bible, you might discover 2 Corinthians 10:4 (KJV), *"For the weapons of our warfare are not carnal, but mighty through God to the pulling down of strongholds."* You might discover Philippians 4:13 (KJV), which says, *"I can do all things through Christ which strengtheneth me."* You might discover Romans 8:28 (KJV), which says, *"And we know that all things work together for good to them that love God, to them who are the called according to his purpose."*

Satan is so afraid that if you read your Bible daily and make reading your Bible a habit, you might discover Matthew 4 and read about how Jesus defeated Satan's temptations. Jesus defeated Satan's temptations! That sounds like something we should look at closer. If Jesus could defeat temptation and The Apostle Paul in 1 Corinthians 11:1 (NIV) says, *"Follow my example, as I follow the example of Christ,"* then that means we are to imitate Christ and do as He did and operate as He did and function as He did and DEFEAT TEMPTATION as He did.

CHAPTER 7

Satan's Plan Versus Jesus' Response

We must examine how Jesus responded to temptation. Jesus' response to temptation lays out for us a blueprint for how we are to respond to temptation. This story of Jesus defeating Satan's temptation is in the books of Matthew (4:1-11), Mark (1:12-13), and Luke (4:1-13). The book of Matthew gives the most details about this event.

Jesus Is Tempted in the Wilderness, Matthew 4:1-11 (NIV)

[1]*"Then Jesus was led by the Spirit into the wilderness to be tempted by the devil.* [2]*After fasting forty days and forty nights, he was hungry.* [3]*The tempter came to him and said, "If you are the Son of God, tell these stones to become bread."*

[4]*Jesus answered, "It is written: 'Man shall not live on bread alone, but on every word that comes from the mouth of God.'"*

[5]*Then the devil took him to the holy city and had him stand on the highest point of the temple.* [6]*"If you are the Son of God," he*

said, "throw yourself down. For it is written: "'He will command his angels concerning you, and they will lift you up in their hands, so that you will not strike your foot against a stone."

[7]Jesus answered him, "It is also written: 'Do not put the Lord your God to the test.'"

[8]Again, the devil took him to a very high mountain and showed him all the kingdoms of the world and their splendor. [9]"All this I will give you," he said, "if you will bow down and worship me."

[10]Jesus said to him, "Away from me, Satan! For it is written: 'Worship the Lord your God and serve him only.'"

[11]Then the devil left him, and angels came and attended him."

The Holy Spirit led Jesus into the wilderness so the devil could tempt Him. The devil's temptations focused on three crucial areas:

- physical desires,
- pride, and
- possessions and power.

Do any of those three areas of temptation sound familiar? Have you ever had temptations that involved your physical desires? Maybe you have had the temptation to eat more than you should. "I am going to get me a piece of that fried chicken." You are already full; you are following your doctor's orders, so you ate the baked chicken instead of the fried chicken. However, Mom's fried chicken looks so good that you cannot resist it, so you crunch down on a big juicy piece.

Have you ever had a temptation that dealt with your pride? "Honey, can you believe he had the nerve to introduce me as plain old John Smith instead of correctly introducing me as the Right Reverend, Apostle, Dr. John Smith? How dare him!"

Have you ever had a temptation that dealt with your wanting to possess more and to gain more power? "I hear that anyone who is anyone lives in that new neighborhood across the street," or, "I think it is time to buy a bigger house. I want to keep up with the Jones family that I heard just moved into those big houses across the street."

How dare the devil try to trick and tempt our Lord and Savior Jesus Christ? If the devil would tempt Jesus, then he will tempt you and me. God gives the devil access to Jesus so he could tempt Him. God gives him access to tempt Jesus just as He gave him access to test Job in the Old Testament. Job 2:3(NIV) says, *"Then the Lord said to Satan, "Have you considered my servant Job?"* Matthew 4:4(NIV) says, *"Then Jesus was led by the Spirit into the wilderness to be tempted by the devil."*

Let me pause right here to remind you that because God has saved you, you now belong to Him and the devil can no longer do whatever he wants to do in your life. God has set limits on what the devil can do in your life. For this reason, we never need to fear the devil or his temptations, even when we feel most attacked by him. Remember that Romans 8:28 (KJV)says, *"And we know that all things work together for good to them that love God, to them who are the called according to his purpose."*

There was a purpose to tempting Jesus. The devil was hoping to tempt and trick Jesus into submitting to him instead of submitting to God. The devil could only tempt Jesus, he could not force Jesus to do anything. God allowed the devil access to His son Jesus to tempt Him because God wants us to see that the "Last Adam," Jesus Christ, can do what the first Adam failed to do, which was to defeat the temptations of the devil.

Now, before we look closer at Jesus' response to temptation, let us examine the devil's timing when he came to tempt Jesus and see if we can learn anything about the enemy's tactics. In Satan's mind, God had given him access to Jesus at the best time. Jesus had eaten nothing for forty days and forty nights. It was clear the devil must have been watching Jesus fast for forty days and forty nights because his first temptation was to tempt Jesus with a physical desire for food. So, the devil says, "Okay, He is physically weak, He is alone, and He was facing the conditions of the wilderness." The devil foolishly mistook Jesus' physical weakness for spiritual weakness. The enemy will attack you with a temptation(s) when he feels you are most vulnerable to his attack. The devil's first temptation would not have been to tempt Jesus to turn stones into bread if Jesus had already eaten a meal and was full. The devil held no concern for Jesus. He did not simply want to make sure

Jesus ate something. He wanted to use physical hunger to trick Jesus into doing something that was the devil's idea. He wanted to see if he could get Jesus to follow his instructions and prove that he was the "Son of God" and perform for the devil. Each of the enemy's temptations for Jesus involved Jesus following the enemy's instructions. The devil wanted Jesus to "turn stones into bread," to "throw himself off the highest point of the temple," and to "bow down and worship Satan." The devil tempted Jesus, and the devil tempts us because He wants us to stop following God and turn control of our lives over to him. When you and I give in to temptation, we allow the tempter or the temptation to take a position of control in our lives. When we give in to temptation and we sin, we are asking God to take a backseat to the temptation and, at that moment, the temptation is our god.

Jesus refused to make God take a backseat, and He refused to allow these enticing temptations to cause Him to sin. It was so important for us that the devil tempted Jesus. By not giving in to temptation, He showed that He was sinless. His temptation was also a perfect model for how we are to handle temptation. Jesus modeled for us how we can face temptation and not give in to the temptation. I used to struggle with Matthew 4:4, where the Spirit (the Holy Spirit) led Jesus into the wilderness so the devil could tempt Him. Understanding this was a struggle. However, I have grown to understand and love what this means: God was always in control and these temptations were a part of His plan for Jesus. It also illustrates how much God loves us, that He would allow Jesus, His only son, to be in a position for the devil to tempt him, for us to learn from the example that Jesus gives us on how to fight temptation.

Now, let us examine how Jesus fights these temptations and defeats the enemy. Notice how after every temptation the devil threw at Jesus, He attacked the devil and the temptation immediately with the word of God. Jesus did not leave to go further into the wilderness to pray more or to fast some more. He did not leave the wilderness to look for the disciples to ask them for help. He did not find some religious leaders like the Pharisees and Sadducees to ask them for help on how to deal with these temptations. Instead, He took immediate action.

Now, let me stop here. There is nothing wrong with prayer and fasting. Prayer and fasting prepare you to do spiritual battle. Through prayer, which is communication with God, we can do as Paul suggests in Ephesians 6:11 (NIV) and *"Put on the full armor of God, so that you can take your stand against the devil's schemes."* Jesus took a stand against the devil's schemes and He took immediate action. He fought the enemy's attacks with his Sword, the word of God. When you are under attack, you must fight back with your Sword. After each temptation, Jesus immediately and automatically fires back at the enemy with

Scriptures. He said repeatedly that "It is written." It is so awesome that Jesus, who is the Word, used the word of God that was already written to defeat the enemy's attacks. He did this because Jesus was validating and illustrating for us the power of God's Word. It is so powerful and has such sustaining power that Jesus quoted from the book of Deuteronomy, which was reportedly written in 1406 BC. It is powerful to note that Scripture written before the birth of Christ has the power to defeat the devil. The Word defeats the devil because the word of God never fades, never gets old, and never loses its power!

God's Word is so powerful, and it is a weapon that the devil cannot fight against. When the devil tempted Jesus, He used the Sword, the word of God, to fight these temptations. Shouldn't we follow this example? I say we absolutely should. Jesus is our perfect example, and His use of the word of God was automatic. Jesus does not hesitate, nor does the Bible record that Jesus had to think about how to respond because His response was automatic. Likewise, our response to temptation, since we are to imitate Jesus, should be automatic. Our response should automatically use one of our greatest weapons to fight the enemy, and this is with the word of God. This explains why the devil does not want us to read, memorize, and make Scripture a part of our daily lives. This explains why the devil's goal is that no one reads the Bible daily because he knows and realizes the power of God's Word. If he can keep the Bible out of our hands and away from our minds, he will strip us of the greatest weapon that is available to us to defeat him and defeat temptation. This also explains why the devil could only tempt Jesus with three temptations. The enemy had to stop because He could not fight against the Sword of the Spirit, which is God's word. Jesus was attacking the enemy with God's Word every time the devil unleashed a temptation. Notice that each temptation was completely different. The devil used a temptation that dealt with a physical desire, and immediately Jesus attacked the enemy and this temptation. Next, the devil used another temptation to entice Jesus into being filled with pride, but immediately Jesus attacked the enemy and this temptation. Last, the devil unleashed a temptation aimed at enticing Jesus with acquiring possessions and gaining power. Again, Jesus immediately attacked the enemy with Scripture. The devil stopped at three temptations because he could no longer stand being attacked by the powerful Sword of God's Word. Finally, Jesus told the devil to get away from Him. The devil left and the temptations ended. If you automatically use the Sword of the Spirit to attack the enemy, temptations will end, forcing the enemy to leave.

You may think, Of course, Jesus automatically recited Scripture and used it as a weapon against the devil, and you are exactly right. John 1 (KJV)says, *"In the beginning was the Word, and the Word was with God and the Word was God."* Jesus was and is the Word and it was and is who He is. It was automatic for Him. His response was automatic. His response was automatic even though He was hungry and even though He was physically weak. His response was automatic despite the devil trying his best efforts to trick and tempt Jesus. Jesus responded in the perfect way to defeat the enemy and the temptations.

The primary goal of this book is to show you how you can copy Jesus and use Scripture to defeat Satan and any temptation and do it automatically. To do this, you must have determination. Determination to no longer allow Satan to win victories in your life. Determination to win with Christ every day. Determination to win against demonic forces that will tempt you to lust, to be envious of others, to be jealous of others, to lie, to steal, to overeat, etc. Determination to win against any enticement that will cause you to sin. Winning against temptation requires us to run in the opposite direction of where the temptation or Satan is trying to lead us. Sometimes we must literally run in the opposite direction, and at other times we must figuratively run to God's Word and use His Word to fight against the temptation. In the Bible, Joseph literally ran away from Potiphar's wife. In Genesis 39, Potiphar's wife targeted young Joseph, Jacob's son, for an adulterous affair. She tempted him day after day, but Joseph held firm to his convictions and rebuffed her advances. Not only did he refuse to go to bed with her, but he wisely refused to "even be with her"

(Genesis 39:10). One day, when no one else was in the house, she caught Joseph and pulled him to her, trying to seduce him: "She caught him by his cloak and said, 'Come to bed with me!' But he left his cloak in her hand and ran out of the house" (verse 12). This is an excellent example of fleeing temptation. Joseph did not stand around to argue or give himself time to reconsider. He fled.[8] Joseph took immediate action!

When tempted, we must take immediate action. Running is an action, and it requires us to move with haste. When facing temptation, we must move with haste. When Satan tempted Jesus, He quickly acted against Satan's temptations. Jesus responded quickly and automatically to Satan's temptations. He did not hesitate. He ran to God's Word and used it against Satan. After every temptation that Satan tried, Jesus used Scripture to attack. So how can we do this? By also running to God's Word and attacking Satan or the temptation with the word of God and doing it automatically as Jesus did.

---

[8]"Flee Temptation." GotQuestions.Org/flee-temptation.html

CHAPTER 8

Armed and Ready

We must remain armed and ready to fight against the devil's schemes and to fight against temptation. I want to arm you with a few practical steps so you will have an automatic response when facing temptation. I am not suggesting these steps are the only way to deal with temptation, but the Lord has led me to write to you about this way. So, here it is. Each morning you start your day in prayer, simply pray and, after giving God thanks, intentionally ask Him to help you defeat temptations. Also, ask God to help you to put on the full armor of God. In Ephesians 6:11 (NIV), Paul encourages us to, *"Put on the full armor of God, so that you can take your stand against the devil's schemes."* We need to put on the full armor of God daily, to do battle against the agenda of Satan. God has already assured us the victory through His son Jesus Christ and has also equipped us with the correct weaponry to fight. Sadly, many Christians lose the daily battle against the devil's schemes because we step on the battlefield of life without the full armor of God and the Sword of the Spirit. We put on the full armor of God through prayer, so starting your day with prayer and asking God for His help is an essential step if you are going to defeat temptation. After prayer, you need to arm yourself with the Sword of the Spirit, which is God's Word the Bible. You must read your Bible daily and I suggest reading your Bible as often as you can each day. Reading your Bible in the morning, specifically asking God to help you put on the full armor of God and His help to defeat temptation, is necessary to equip you for the day ahead. Trust me, you will not find the time in the morning to read and pray. You must intentionally make the time, and this might require that you get up a little earlier, but it will be well worth it. As you read the Bible, read to learn more about God and read to find Scriptures that you can take with you to fight against the enemy's schemes and temptation.

A favorite Scripture I take with me every day is Psalm 23:1(KJV), *"The Lord is my shepherd; I shall not want."* I've committed this Scripture to memory. Memorizing Scripture is important. The late Billy Graham said, "I am convinced that one of the greatest things we can do is to memorize Scriptures." Pastor and author John Piper expounds on memorizing Scripture when he says that, "Memorizing Scriptures enables me to hit the devil in the face with a force he can't resist to protect myself and my family from his assaults." Psalm 23:1 helps me "hit the devil in the face" and attack his schemes and temptations. I love this popular Scripture because it reminds me that I am dependent on the Lord, He is in control, and I am to follow Him and remember that He is my provider. It reminds me that if I am following the Lord, I am heading in the right direction. I use this Scripture to fight temptation when I am tempted to follow things that do not line up with God's Word. For example, when I am tempted to gamble and buy a lottery ticket when the jackpots are the highest, I fight that temptation by reminding myself that "The Lord is my Shepard; I shall not want." When I am tempted, I will say, "The Lord is my Shepard; I shall not want to buy lottery tickets." In this way, I have personalized the Scripture and used it to specifically attack the temptation that I am facing. I use Scripture to remind myself of the truth. When I am tempted to worry about a situation I am facing, I arm myself with a Scripture like Luke 12:25-26 (NIV) where Jesus says, "Who of you by worrying can add a single hour to your life? Since you cannot do this very little thing, why do you worry about the rest?" When I feel unqualified for something or when I feel inadequate, I arm myself with a Scripture like Philippians 4:13 (KJV)that says, "I can do all things through Christ which strengtheneth me." I arm myself with Scripture to attack anything trying to get me to feel, think, express, or believe something contrary to the word of God. This has proven to be a powerful method for fighting back against the devil and even against misguided thoughts.

Just as buying a lottery ticket, feeling inadequate, or worrying can be on my list of temptations that I need Scripture to defeat, you may also have a list of temptations you need to defeat. Except for God, no one knows you better than you know yourself. You know that, for example, jealousy, lust, or smoking cigarettes is a temptation for you. Avoid being prideful and admit to yourself and to God (who already knows) a list of your temptations. Ask God to help you defeat these things. It is okay to be vulnerable and truthful with God. He already knows what you are struggling with and He wants to help you.

God helps us by giving us His Word to be used as a weapon to attack temptations. When temptation comes your way, attack it with the word of God. For example, if smoking cigarettes is a temptation for you, then every time the enemy temps you with a cigarette, you might recite or think about one of my go-to Scriptures Psalm 23:1, "The Lord is my Shepherd; I shall not want." Or maybe recite or think about 1 Corinthians 6:19-20 (NIV)that says, *"Do you not know that your bodies are temples of the Holy Spirit, who is in you, whom you have received from God? You are not your own; you were bought at a price. Therefore, honor God with your bodies."* Smoking does not honor God with your body, so you must defeat the temptation of smoking. Every time you think about or are tempted with cigarettes, attack the enemy and this temptation with the word of God. Every time you see an advertisement for cigarettes or every time you see someone smoking a cigarette, recite Psalms 23:1 or 1 Corinthians 6:19-20. Make a habit of repeatedly reciting Scripture. I do not advocate smoking, but if you give in to the temptation, recite the word of God. Find a Scripture and attack that which is attacking you. Continue to attack that temptation with the word of God. Eventually, after twenty-one days after the temptation comes, you are going to form an automatic habit of attack. You are going to form a habit of attacking that temptation with the word of God. After sixty-three days, your brain is going to write code that says when you are tempted with cigarettes, you automatically attack the temptation with the word of God. It will become automatic for you and the very temptation the devil thought he would use to destroy you, will be the same temptation to lead you automatically to the word of God and the freedom from cigarettes and temptation that the Bible offers. The enemy's plan of attack will backfire, and instead of the temptation for cigarettes making you run to grab a cigarette, now it will make you run to grab the word of God. The devil will be forced to stop using the temptation of cigarettes to attack you because you have formed a habit and your brain has written a code that automatically attacks the enemy, the temptation, and the sin of smoking cigarettes. I promise you that like Jesus in Matthew 4:10, you will be able to recite the Bible and say, "Away from me, Satan!" Satan will flee because he cannot fight against the word of God. Just as Satan left Jesus and stopped trying to tempt Him. Satan will leave and stop trying to tempt you with cigarettes. He will leave because he will realize that every time, he tries to tempt you with cigarettes, he gets attacked with the word of God. Satan cannot fight against the word of God. Satan will realize that he will have to try something else because cigarettes are only driving this man or woman to the word of God and his attempt to tempt him or her with cigarettes is causing him to be attacked.

Satan wants to harm and attack you, but he does not want you to attack him. God is so powerful, He can take you from being a victim of a satanic attack or stronghold and place you in your intended position as a winner by giving you victory over the enemy. I like what Genesis 50:20 says, "You intended to harm me, but God intended it for good to accomplish what is now being done, the saving of many lives." God wants to give you victory so your testimony and work in service to Him can save the lives of many others. This is the reason drugs did not kill you. This is the reason cancer could not stop you. This is the reason lust could no longer consume you. This is the reason racism could not oppress you. God is in control and has other plans for your life. His plans are for your good and your benefit. He wants you to grow in your relationship with Him so He can give your life purpose and meaning.

Now, remember the science I told you about in Chapter 6, where you form a habit in twenty-one days and your brain writes code in sixty-three days. Remember, this is how you make things happen as automatically as breathing or your heart beating. Well, I have tried the very things I am teaching you in my own life, and I have found that the God we serve is not bound by the rules of science or by anything. I found that what science and my research said would take twenty-one and sixty-three days to accomplish, God has and is accomplishing and freeing me from the temptations and strongholds I thought I would always have to struggle with. I want you to try the steps I have given you on how to defeat temptation, but do not be surprised if God does something unexpected in your life, because of your willingness to follow Jesus' example of how to defeat temptation. Beloved friend, the power is not in the method I have given you. Please remember the power to defeat temptation belongs to God and He alone gives you the power to escape temptation and to run to Him. The power to use Scripture as a weapon can only come from God and it can only be utilized by those who belong to God.

The seven sons of Sceva made the mistake of trying to use Jesus' name like magic words used in a magician's trick. This story is found in Acts 19:11-20. There was a Jewish high priest named

Sceva who had seven sons. His seven sons were traveling exorcists. In the city of Ephesus, God was performing many miraculous things through the Apostle Paul. God had given Paul the power to cast out demons using the name of Jesus. The seven sons of Sceva saw Paul do this and they tried to imitate Paul. They would say, in Acts 19:13 (NIV), *"In the name of the Jesus whom Paul preaches, I command you to come out."* One day they tried this, and the demon answered them, in Acts 19:15 (NIV), saying, *"Jesus I know, and Paul I know about, but who are you?"* The man who had the demon jump on them, severely injured the seven brothers and they ran out of the house, bleeding and naked. I mention this, one of my favorite biblical stories, because it is a warning and a reminder that the power to defeat Satan and temptation does not belong to a method, but God. God is our power source, and you cannot have victory over temptation and use His Word to defeat temptation without having access to His power. To have access to His power you must belong to Him, you must be saved.

If you belong to God, then I pray your perspective on why God allows temptation will change. God ultimately allows temptation to come into your life because He wants you to grow in your faith to a place where you put Him first even over your own enticing desires. He allows temptation to come so He can allow you to imitate His Son Jesus Christ and use His Word to defeat the tempter and defeat the temptation. God wants you to imitate Jesus so there can be no mistake it was God who gave you the power to fight and defeat temptation. The power to defeat temptation can only come from God and He alone deserves the credit. It is His "full armor of God" that allows us to protect ourselves and our families and allows us the ability to fight.

I hope you will show God how grateful you are for His love by committing your life to serve Him and leading others to a relationship with Him. Tell your family and friends, co-workers, neighbors, and strangers about the impact a relationship with Jesus Christ has had on your life. Tell others how God set you free from a gambling stronghold. Tell others how God set you free from giving in to the temptation of premarital sex. Tell others how God delivered you from jealousy, pride, gossiping, and cursing. I promise you if you do this, your life will automatically be filled with joy. You will automatically love others when they hate you. You will automatically have peace amid a storm. You will automatically have victory because of our Lord and Savior Jesus Christ!

Dear Reader,

I sincerely want to thank you for reading my book. Keep reading, you have one more chapter to go. I hope that you are enjoying the book and are finding some tools to help you grow in your relationship with Christ.

I want to ask you something. Will you give Automatic a review on Amazon.com? Ninety-three percent of customers will read online reviews before they purchase a product. Your review could be the push a potential reader needs to pick up their own copy of Automatic and begin to defeat temptation.

I would be so grateful for your review and I am excited to read it. Thanks!

–Aswin

A Preemptive Strike

My final push for you is that you will grow to a place where God becomes first in your life over everything else. My final prayer is that your thoughts and actions automatically line up with the truth and instructions of God's Word. My final opinion is that I believe God wants you to grow to a place where you are not only reacting automatically to fight against the enemy when he launches an attack at you, but I pray that you grow to a place in your relationship with God where you launch a preemptive strike against the enemy. A preemptive strike is a surprise attack launched before an enemy's expected attack on you. My prayer is that you grow to a place where the devil hates to see you coming because everything about you represents Christ. I pray that you grow to a place where you take Jesus seriously and are a true ambassador for Him here on the Earth. I pray that you will put on the full armor of God through prayer and begin to ask God where He wants you to fight and how He would like to use you to strike a blow against the enemy. It is not by accident that you are reading this book. God wants to use you to strike the enemy through prayer and to strike the enemy with God's Word. You can preemptively strike the enemy by attacking him before he attacks you.

Sadly, my parents got divorced when I was seven years old. Their divorce was the first divorce in my immediate family. After the divorce, my grandmother and my mother, who are women of faith, got together and prayed. They prayed for me and my brother. My brother was eleven and I was seven. Of course, at this young age, we were not married and were not even thinking about marriage, but they prayed for our future marriages. They prayed for our future wives and families. They prayed and asked God to not allow the devil to cause our marriages to end in divorce. In this way, they were launching a preemptive strike against the plans of the enemy. To this day, both my brother and I, by God's grace, are still married, with each of us soon to celebrate twenty years of marriage. Satan wanted to create a pattern of divorce in my family, but I believe God honored my grandmother's and mother's prayers and has not allowed the enemy's destructive plan to work because they struck him first. They prayed proactively instead of reactively. This allowed them to launch a preemptive strike. Jesus launched a preemptive strike against Satan in Luke 22:31-32(NIV). The Bible says, "*Simon, Simon, Satan has asked to sift all of you as wheat. But I have prayed for you, Simon, that your faith may not fail. And when you have turned back, strengthen your brothers."* Jesus prayed for Simon, who would later be named Peter and by doing so, He preemptively struck Satan who wanted to destroy Peter's faith. Jesus says, *"But I have prayed for you."* Jesus strikes Satan's destructive plan.

Beloved reader, my final desire is that you imitate Jesus and pray and thereby preemptively strike Satan's plans of destruction for your families, your neighbors, your country, and this world. Satan wants to destroy our faith in God, but as I write these words, I am praying, and I am imitating Jesus, and I am asking God to not allow your faith to fail. I know God will answer this prayer and I am encouraging you to now "strengthen your brothers and sisters," by praying for their futures, that their faith will not fail. By doing this you will launch a preemptive strike against Satan, which I believe will automatically change the future.

Notes

Notes

Notes

Notes

Notes

Notes

Notes

Made in the USA
Monee, IL
18 May 2021